On the Road
to
Ollantaytambo

Ian Beech

On the Road
to
Ollantaytambo

Ian Beech

Poetry Island Press

This edition published by Poetry Island Press 2015

Poetry Island Press
29 Dean Street, Crediton, EX17 3EN

ISBN 978-0-9933961-0-6

Printed by www.lulu.com

For Maria

August 2015

Heartfelt thanks to all those who have helped make this volume possible: my muse Maria for her love, support, belief and not least patience, my daughters Emily, Grace and Megan for inspiring me and tolerating my efforts, oldest friend David for providing me with plenty of poetic ammunition, Iris and Terry whose friendship has sustained me through the years, poetry hosts John Stuart, Alasdair Paterson, Gemma Green and Liz Adams, Tim King and Morwenna Alldis, Robert Garnham, Chris Brooks and Ian Royce Chamberlain for all giving me a chance – and inviting me back, all my friends, family and the fellow South West poets who have offered encouragement and friendship over the last three years.

Special thanks to Tim King for technical computer support, as well as for reading my draft manuscript and making various helpful suggestions (many of which I have adopted) and to Robert Garnham for reading my draft manuscript, losing his notes and only remembering that he thought I should ensure the cover was waterproof …

Many thanks also to marvellous artist Jo Mortimer for the Poetry Island Press logo, adapted from the logo she created for Poetry Island at The Blue Walnut Cafe, Torquay, transforming my scribbled ideas into a beautiful work of art. The other talented member of the household, poet and novelist Paul Mortimer, has my sincere gratitude for his advice on avoiding potential litigation, which resulted in me removing one short poem from the book 'just in case'.

Finally, I must mention the proprietors of the venue that has become my spiritual home, The Blue Walnut Cafe in Torquay: initially Gary and Debbie Whyte and currently Dave, Jane & Dj Schofield. Thank you all for making the The Blue Walnut such a brilliant venue in which to perform.

Contents

Sally

It started at the ice-rink on that school trip.
Two sixth-formers holding hands to stay upright,
Failing and falling before the end of the evening,
Crashing into the slush,
Your clothes wet through,
Mine completely dry,
Due to the double bonus
Of falling on top of you.

Ten weeks of teenage romance
Before the day your mother
Died at the wheel,
Driving home to Llangollen,
Still in her fiftieth year.
I'm so glad that I knew her, if briefly.

Two perplexed seventeen-year-olds,
We stumbled on,
But you needed to be with your father
And we slowly drifted apart.

Much later, when a student in Liverpool,
You wrote to me,
A student in Exeter,
And said that you missed me.
Older and marginally wiser,
We resumed our youthful romance,
Both of us glad of a second chance.

I remember so clearly
How we converged on the corner
Of Bridge Street.
You burst into view,
A vision of perfect young womanhood,
Strikingly exquisite in the bloom
Of your twenty-first summer.

Love and young man's vanity
Coursed through my veins at the sight:
Beautiful, long tall Sally,
Happy and proud to be meeting me.

Two hundred miles can take their toll
And before New Year, 'we' were no more.

You were exactly four weeks younger than me,
Then.
But much as I hoped to,
I never saw you again.
The regular call home
From the red, Rhyl, November 'phone box
Brought the news that I could scarcely believe.

Now you have had nearly thirty-five years
Head start on eternity.
I have some photographs
And memories engraved deep inside my heart.
One day my girls may find your letter,
When they inherit their mother's loft.

But I know that however long I may live,
I shall never forget you.
Beautiful Sally, who had so much to give,
But who never reached twenty-two.

Amo, Amas, Amat

Amo, Amas, Amat.
I should use conjugate
But it seems sadly inappropriate.
So, I am declining 'To Love'
As you are declining my love.

I'm too young you say. Too young at 55?
My last flush of youth a distant memory.

Surely these are not **your** declining years.
'Age cannot wither her, nor custom stale
Her infinite variety' claimed the bard.
Yet by you, my love, my love is barred.

Yes, I'm tense. Past, barely present,
Certainly imperfect, but not future.
And so I am declining 'To Love'
As you are declining my love.

Time passes so swiftly.
We are both declining, my love.
And you are still declining my love.
So with all hope now gone,
My love is slowly declining, my love.

3.10a.m. 4th August 2012
First draft written while unable to sleep

For Maria

Enchanted Evenings, Ancient Games

The world focuses on London
But my eyes are elsewhere.

First sight – across a crowded room.
They said you are from Exeter.
Disappointment for me.
If not outside my league,
Most definitely within
My double-dip, petrol budget exclusion zone.

Second sight – and first conversation.
In so many ways, you are closer to home
Than I had thought possible.
Voice of an angel, personality to match.
'You remember me', said with naïve girlish charm,
Disarming me at a stroke.

Assuredly, desire at third sight – if not before.
You touched my arm and I touched yours.
Attraction most delightfully confirmed,
Neither of us concerned which prying eyes
Discerned the growing flame.

I've suffered torch-bearing ennui of late
But the ancient game is now afoot once more.
No time for track and field
As to your kiss I yield.
No stately, pointless dressage –
You vault into my arms.

Wow!
A magnificent,
Unforgettable
Opening
Ceremony.

There may be hurdles to surmount
Before our race is run.
The ultimate prize may remain,
Tantalisingly, beyond our reach.
You're a glass-half-full kind of girl,
And I've always wondered
When I'll find a glass round here.

So 100 metres – or marathon?
That is the question.
Only time will tell.

Oh, the resilience of the human heart!
I have no medals to bestow
But these golden sunflowers express my hopes
And who knows where they may lead …?

Maria Moore: What's in a Name?

I've just met you.
A girl named Maria.
♪ *And suddenly I find*
I've lost my peace of mind ♪ –
I lie awake in bed
With West Side Story in my head.

And you are Moore by name,
More still by nature.
Our greedy eyes
Devour each other without shame,
Consensual, contextual obscenities inflame,
Life-affirming passion our new game
And no two times are ever quite the same.

Oh, this raging torrent cannot last.
We'll shoot our rapids, paddling fast.
Calmer waters lie downstream,
Deeper channels yet undreamed.
Hand in hand, towards the sea.
More of you? More of me?
More of us?
Let's wait and see.

Slippers

No pipes, no papers.
It's 2012, not 1952.
Fear not, no unreconstructed
Drudgery for you.

BUT

You wish to buy me slippers
To wear upon your floors.
How sweet the thoughts of pre-love.
My eyes detect no flaws.
I barely see the doors
You lock behind,
Confirming my confinement
Of the sweetest kind,
Solitary no more,
Barefooted captive on your floor.

Death by Chocolate

My first cake baked, aged 55.
Just chocolate cake, no frills.
How have I stayed alive
Without such basic skills?

Ancient knowledge passed on
From generation to generation,
Now handed up from child to parent,
From kindly daughter to untutored sire.

Mind you, ingredients to sink a battleship.
Cholesterol gone wild.
A culinary arms race filled my bowl,
Vessel-clogging pleasure its wanton goal.
Blair's missing link? Lifted when it cooled,
A weapon of mass destruction from a rack.

This will put my bypass to the test.
My heart's assailed by cake and love.
To which will I succumb?
My daughter smiles,
Gently tolerating my autumnal passion
For love new-found.
No youthful snigger as I fashion
A chocolate buttercream heart to surmount
My latest pride and joy.

Before the transport of delight –
The Cakeman cometh.
Delivered with a kiss
By this newly-trained
Purveyor of domestic bliss.
Even Nigella can't do this …

All's fair in love and war.
Served on a plate right inside your door.
One small slice, exquisite taste
Or maybe just une petite more …

'Don't eat it all at once', I say.
'Let's live to feast another day.'

Speed Dating

First contact,
Non-verbal contract,
Swiftly signed and sealed.
Intentions instantly revealed,
Both of us quite sure
We've never wanted more.
Locked inside your door,
Two hearts beat all aquiver
And so anxious to deliver.
There's no more to be said
As we sleep on your bed.

Beyond the Call of Duty

You won the Military Medal, in Bellenglise, Picardy,
Six weeks before the end of the Great War.
Still plenty of time for comrades to be slaughtered.
Sapper James Beech, laying cable,
Exposed overnight near enemy lines,
Under heavy shellfire for several hours.
The framed portrait tells the tale
That you never mentioned.
You avoided your own violent death,
Returned to the pit and to share Violet's life,
Married to her for 53 years.
But they don't give medals for that.

The Telegram

Stood outside the house when the telegram arrived,
Grandpa opened it and seemed satisfied.
'She's staying in Bournemouth for another two weeks.'

Grandma Beech loved her tennis.
British Hard Court Championships every year.
'Next best thing to Wimbledon.'
She'd stay on with her friends
And make a full five weeks of it.

Gramp, meanwhile, would choose
His fortnight in Blackpool strategically,
Careful not to overlap,
Anxious to enjoy the benefits of the bracing sea air
And a full seven weeks' remission.

Seaside Postcards

The annual ritual:
Grandpa's postcards from Blackpool.
Donkeys, the pier, the tower.
We received them all in turn.

In the early days
They were positively garrulous:
'Dear Ian and Pat
The weather's fine.
Having a great time.
Lots of love, Grandpa xxx'.

In later years, time had tamed
Your loquacious nature.
Biro ink at a premium,
Your missive had shrunk to
'Lots of love, Gramp'.

What you got up to
In your two weeks of freedom,
We never knew.
I hope you had a truly great time,
Whatever the weather.

By your final holiday,
You had perfected
The art of postcard writing.
In addition to the donkey and the stamp,
Love summed up in just one word: 'Gramp'.

The Parting

Wind blowing litter
In the Liverpool street
Where we parked.
Flowers on sale
By the hospital door.
Winter trips to Sefton General.

On our last visit,
Dad visibly shocked
By your condition,
Even this teenage boy
Aware there was no hope.

Dad took his comb
And gently groomed your hair.
A last act of love by a man
Fate forced into a tank,
Towards a man
Fate forced into a trench,
United by untold memories.

Dad

Downstairs in our council house home in North Wales,
If not in the hall,
You were either in the kitchen or 'the other room'.
Through the haze of time,
I recall a moment that changed my life.

When you are twenty-one you're too young
To know the unuttered words that left unsaid
You'll live to regret decades later.
Home from university, full of ideas, hormones,
All-knowing confidence – and youthful insensitivity.

My parents with early morning and full working day ahead.
Me – slouched in front of the late night film,
To while away the early hours before
Another aimless day begun at noon.

I still see him stood in the doorway,
About to climb the stairs,
Pausing and saying to me,
'Goodnight, Ian.'

'Goodnight', my good-natured but brief reply,
Eyes returning to the flickering screen.

But he did not move.

I turned and saw his saddened eyes
And then he slowly spoke.
'You never call me Dad.'

Surprised, I managed
'Oh, sorry. Goodnight, Dad.'
He smiled, glanced away and left.

Men of his generation kept their feelings battened down,
As if emotional emancipation and literacy
Had yet to be invented.
He learned to drive in a tank and seldom spoke
Of all he witnessed in 1944 and '45.
Not forgotten but buried.

Sometimes we learn the truth when we least expect it.
He would never dream of saying 'I love you'
To his full-grown son.
Never again did I fail to acknowledge
His poignant, proud paternity.
Yes, I always called him 'Dad' from that day on –
And still do all these years later, though he is now long gone.

So, here's to the Stoke City FA Cup Final you dreamed of –
And incredibly I have seen –
And my three precious daughters
You would have bounced upon your knee.

Now I know what you felt.
I hope they will always call me 'Dad'.

Late

Today's not a day for me to be late.
How many buses and trains
Have I missed down the years
And heard your patient entreaties
For me to plan my time better?

It's taking too long to buy these shoes,
From a man who's known you for decades
But doesn't know you have a family.
Professional detachment, I suppose.
He probably doesn't know that you despise
Winston Churchill, Margaret Thatcher
And Alf Ramsey,
Though many people do.

You see, it's just that I'll need these new shoes
To accompany you tomorrow.

Finally, off to the hospital
For our last face-to-face meeting.
I'm not quite on time
But it is you who is truly late
And now will be so for evermore.

They warn me of slight bruising on your face,
Where your head hit the bedside cabinet as you fell.
I steel myself for this new, untimely experience,
With a heady cocktail of contradictory emotions:
I'm gripped by numbness and pain,
Fear and fascination.

I step into the room and there you aren't,
The recognisable shell of the father I loved so much.
The bruising is minimal and untroubling
But I'm struck by the total,
Irreversible, absence of you.
You are not sleeping:
You are gone.

I sense how others may conjure
The parting of spirit from body
And imagine a flight of fancy
To a Greater Beyond.
That's not for me.

I'm content that it will not be you
We consign to the flames tomorrow.
I see that your moment has passed
With a finality that brooks no mediation,
No hope of reunion, just memories,
Until my own instant is history.

Quiet contemplation by your mortal remains,
Your arm cold to the touch.
I softly kiss your forehead,
Below your silvering, receding hairline,
Take one last lingering look,
Then leave.

Just Desserts: a Gastronomic Haiku

Seventeen sylla-
Bubs is too many desserts.
No wonder I'm ill.

Vaulting Ambitions

When I was young I wanted to be a gymnast.
I was always jumping up and down.
I wasn't at all inhibited
But opportunities were strictly limited
Because we lived in a one-horse town.

When I was young I wanted to be an astronaut,
Exploring new worlds for the human race.
But the problem with that?
We lived in a small, if very clean flat.
We had a vacuum but we just didn't have the space.

When I was young I wanted to be a boxer
But I was decidedly meek and frankly too weak
To inflict any damage to eyebrow or cheek.
The trouble with me, you see,
Is that I sting like a butterfly and float like a bee.

When I was young I wanted to be an actor.
I loved Hamlet, Lear and poetry.
But you should've seen how mum leered at me
When I said I wanted to be a Thespian.
She said 'It's physically impossible, Ian.'
And my dad, he seemed to be sneering.
Mind you, they were both hard of hearing.

Escape from Knightshayes

We'd been 'wearing purple' that day,
As Jenny Joseph might say.

Enjoying the sun far too long,
We hadn't thought anything wrong.
Writing and reading my verse,
We'd become Adam and Eve in reverse.
For begging the National Trust's pardon,
We'd got locked inside of its garden.

Fully clothed, not a fig leaf in sight,
We seemed destined to stay there all night.
I said 'What on earth can we do?
I'm sorry, I haven't a clue.'
Maria's reply? 'Just use our common sense.
We'll have to jump over that fence.'

I went first and fell on my back with a crack.
Maria thought she'd need to send for a hearse.
But that flattened clump of bluebells
Sadly fared much worse.
I picked myself up and helped Maria
Get her leg over in a National Trust garden
(Something I never expected to do).
But well, if you were me, wouldn't you?
And she collapsed into my arms
With her delicate charms
And our dream of escape came true.

But I think I ought to mention,
It was hardly my intention,
As I'd jumped, I'd collided with the railings
And I'm really not that partial to 'impalings'.
Since then life's never been the same for us,
Though I don't like to make a fuss.
At least, I'm a fully-paid-up member of the National Truss.

Capitalism for Beginners in Lingua Franca

Steeped in debt, cold and wet, it couldn't get much **D**anker

And it's a fair bet that all our trees are getting **C**anker.

I'm so depressed and my hair is growing **L**anker.

I'm not looking at my best and it's warmer climes for which I **H**anker,

As we curse and nurse our lonely halves in 'The No Hope and **A**nchor'.

'Things could be much worse' my girlfriend says
And for that thought I have to **T**hank her.

She's great – my number one is how I'd **R**ank her.
She says 'Why don't we just hitch a lift on some passing fishing boat
Or **T**anker?'

'Jamaica?' 'No, I wouldn't have to **Y**ank her.'

Ah, but, that ship, just our luck
If something went and **S**ank her,
Somewhere off the coast of Spain
And we missed that midnight train
En route to **S**alamanca.

Ah, but it's all just dreams,
For it clearly seems
My cheque book couldn't be much **B**lanker –
Unless I pulled a highly fraudulent **F**lanker.

No, we'll never mix
With the likes of Mick Jagger
Or even Eastenders' own **B**ianca.

There'll be no Taj Mahal for us, no long-haul planes.
We'll just have to sit at home, and meditate to the strains
Of Ravi **S**hankar.

We won't even 'Always have Paris',
As they say in Casablanca.

My German astrophysicist friend,
A real life Jodrell-Banker,
He'll be political to the end.
Kurt's aptly named for speaking plain
As he tries to explain.

In fact, he couldn't be much Franker,
Danke,

In words often tinged with anger and with Rancour.
He says it always is the same
As he lays all the blame

At the door of each Investment Banker,
Sadly, not hanging out to dry or tied-up to a stake
But sunning himself on some month-long break

In somewhere like Sri Lanka.

Well, no doubt I'm nearly through.
Apologies if I've forgotten anything that might seem obvious to you.
But I simply haven't got the time
To invent a twenty-third rhyme,

As I fear, like that cheque book, my mind is growing Blanker.

Small Arms

Blessed are the Peacebreakers,
For they have inherited the earth.

640 million small arms in the world.
That's pistols, rifles, machine guns, grenade launchers
And all things nice,
Each manufactured to be
A perfect killing device.

640 million small arms in the world.
How many small arms
Have you torn from their mothers' breast
And tossed those babes in pits
Alongside all the rest?

640 million small arms in the world,
Sold by men without a care,
Like breakfast foods or Tupperware.
You men in sharp suits, good at figures,
Although your fingers aren't pulling triggers,
You are the true serial killers.
You have no share
In our anger, horror and despair.

You have a thin veneer of sincere urbanity,
No obvious signs of crazed insanity
To excuse your heinous abuse of humanity.
Your lust for wealth you cannot sate,
Indifferent to horrific scenes,
Your motto: *If you supply the hate,*
Then we'll supply the means.

One person killed every minute with small arms,
In city streets or burned-out farms,

To feed your greed,
You sick death-dealers,
Facilitators of Hell.

Well,
Kiss your lovers, hug your children, greet a friend,
Without a thought of how – and why – lives end.
You rationalise your part in why men kill:
'If we don't sell, then others will.'

Your self-justifying sophistry
Simply doesn't wash with me.
I have **you** in **my** telescopic sights.
Will that give **you** sleepless nights?

You're lucky. I'm not a violent type.
This is just a verbal snipe.
You don't need to lie awake
Terrified of a late night raid by me.
No, you haven't got to quake.
What's there to fear from mere poetry?

So, you'll sleep easy in your beds,
The sleep of the just
Plain Evil.

Oh yes, but please, perchance to dream
And hear those little children scream,
The most searing indictment
Of your deadly, vile incitement
Of crimes of unadulterated hate:
Your small arms used to kill, to maim and violate.
Perhaps imagine **your** loved ones dead,
Shot through stomach, heart or head
And naked on the pyre crudely hurled
And see our protest banner now unfurled
Against you and 640 million small arms in the world.

The Wrong Trousers

Numbingly cold,
The last January day of 1976.
British Rail,
Exeter to Wolverhampton
For the day.

Canal frozen solid on the stretch
Beyond Birmingham,
Adding natural beauty
To the rust-ridden decay,
In the sprawling wasteland
Of the still pre-post-industrial
West Midlands.

Met on Wolverhampton Station
By parents, sister and best friends,
And told by my mother
'You can't go to the football
Wearing those trousers.'

Ashamed by my sartorial inelegance,
I was frog-marched directly to C&A.
I recall dad slipped on the ice
And nearly went under a taxi
While we were making our way.

A nineteen year-old innocent,
Comfortable in my faded bottle-green cords,
Unaware that Molineux was the new Milan,
I meekly submitted,
Rebellion still not even
A twinkle in my eye.

Wolves won 2-1.
My Uncle Tom apologised to us
For his team's success.

'Sorry, but we need the points, Ed.'
They still went down.

I left my nearest and dearest,
Newly-sensibly-trousered,
With another defeat under my belt,
Reflecting that mum would
Probably be disappointed
If my trousers were not
Appreciatively mentioned
In the Sunday match reports.

It wasn't until much later
That I finally went off the rails ...

Homage to Catalunya

I remember it well.
November 1988,
Barcelona v Real Murcia,
When Gary Lineker
Scored twice
On my honeymoon ...
You can still watch it on YouTube.

I'm not married now.

For David

Away Days

The Molineux Express has been cancelled.
It will no longer call at:

Liverpool
Manchester
Newcastle
Or Stoke-upon-Trent.

And not even at:

Blackpool
Bolton
Burnley
Or Ipswich.

Any remaining passengers are asked to transfer to
The slow-train calling at:

Walsall
Crawley
Shrewbury
And Stevenage.

These will now have to do
As Wolves try to avoid a hiding,
In some dismal railway siding,
By the Alex boys in Crewe.

Sadly, there'll be no more trips to Sunderland or Southampton,
Due to a catastrophic points failure at Wolverhampton.

Football on the Quantocks

One fresh spring morning, I set off for work.
Driving from Norton Fitzwarren
Over the Quantocks to Spaxton.

So good to be alive,
As I headed through Kingston St Mary,
Nestled below the slopes.
The roadside stream shimmering and dancing
In the new-found sun,
The banks festooned with primroses
And the promise of more to come.
I spotted rabbits and proud pheasants,
Iridescent-faced survivors
Of the winter chills.
The sharp ascent to The Pines,
Hill-top café, sentinel over the Bristol Channel,
With a hazy hint of Wales beyond.

Down to Spaxton Playing Field
For the Big Match:

Spaxton Under-12s
v
Galmington Dragons Under-12s.

Team shots taken,
Hands shaken,
With acquaintances of long-standing.
(I've done this job for many years,
Promoting the game I love
Through the regional press).

Despite the biting wind on this very sunny day,
I reflected on the innocent joy of youth:
Warming up, receiving tactical advice
From coaches, at least one of whom
Will be a player's mum or dad.

Told I trust 'Play to win but play fair
And, of paramount importance,
Enjoy it and express yourselves.'

Playing organised eleven-a-side league football,
On pitches complete with posts and nets,
In vibrant, sponsored kits
And with an official smart
In his referee's whistle and flute.
All this in such an idyllic setting,
Where greater poets have found inspiration,
High above Bridgwater Bay.

When I was their age, there was one school team.
If you weren't selected, that was that –
Apart from disorganised free-for-alls
On the local rec., pullovers for goals.
We didn't have annual trophy presentations
At local luxury hotels.
But in all truth, we still had lots of fun.

As I drove home contentedly,
Thinking there must be much worse ways
Of not quite earning a living,
I reflected that I watched them without envy,
Glad for the opportunities they seize as of right.
These are their golden days.
Surely, they cannot yet conceive
How lucky they are to be alive,
To be young and to be playing
Football on the Quantocks.

The Joy of House Sharing

When we first met
My sweet, little pet,
I barely gave you a second glance.
My eyes were set on steamy romance.
They weren't inclined to roam
From she with whom you share your home.

But as time went by
You really caught my eye.
When I saw you standing there
In your long black coat,
Looking oh so fair,
It's then my heart you smote.

I loved your long dark hair
And those gorgeous henna streaks contrasting there.
Your lithe and supple body was just wonderful to see.
You started to exert a real hold on me.
With your gentle face so sweet and kind,
Thoughts of you started preying on my mind.

With my feelings I bravely fought.
I didn't think I was that sort.
But you really gave me pause for thought
And all my self-denial came to naught.

I didn't know it would go so far,
And though it seems a shade bizarre,
We now have a marvellous ménage à trois.

Yes, you finally won my heart.
Now I know we three will never part.
My arms round you I'll wrap,
As you sit upon my lap.
I'm learning how to make you purr,
As I stroke your jet black fur.

I can't be clearer than that:
How I love my girlfriend's … cat.

And I hate to be too greedy
But I can be rather needy.
Before I'm too old, I'd love to have
Just one more kitten on our mat
And then we'd have the perfect ménage à quatre.

Hot in Bed

Neither of us is getting any younger,
But you're really hot in bed.
And so am I, it has to be said.
They say 'Many an old fiddle will still
Play an exceptionally fine tune'
But I think it's due, I must entreat,
To that hot-water bottle by your feet,
Even though it's nearly June.

Mornings Can Be Difficult

'It's time to get up!'
'It's time to get up!'
You're telling me, sweetheart.
You're desperate for your breakfast cup
But all I want to do is tup.
Of that you're having none.
In fact, you've upped and gone.
You've started on the toast and jam.
Damn, oh damn, oh damn.
Sometimes it's so hard to be a man.
Oh well, I guess it's time to get up.

Dust to Dust:
The Lament of the Unpublished Poet

My friends have told me once again
That I've become extremely vain.
They say it isn't down to luck
That I haven't got a book.

I send my poems to each big name,
Anticipating instant fame,
But the answer's always just the same.
To my ego it's becoming destructive,
Mind you, they're always polite and constructive.

Why, just the other day,
In a very pleasant way,
One wrote to say
'There's absolutely no chance
Of us making a six-figure advance.
You should just be proud
To read your stuff out loud.
And please don't be fazed
If we listen through windows triple-glazed.

We've got so many manuscripts gathering dust
That we'll make you an offer that's a must, we trust.
Frankly, your 'book' would never be a mover,
So next time, please don't parcel up your oeuvre.
If you really want to clean up and avoid a life of penury,
Then just pop round with your Dyson or your Henry.'

Excess Male

When Patricia threw out her husband,
She then destroyed all of his clothes.
She said 'Good riddance!
I never want another of those.
I'll buy myself a small red van
And a sweet little black and white cat.'
Thereafter, she lived most happily
And we all called her Post-Man Pat.

My First Review

I've just had my first review.
And even though I say so myself,
It wasn't bad …

My first review, my first review!
It's amazingly exciting and all so new.
I'll give it much more than a cursory view.
It's great to read about the success
Of the event in which I sought to impress.
It's a great review!
I'm not actually mentioned – or my verse,
So I guess it could have been far, far worse.
My heartfelt thanks go out to you.
Some other critics, they don't have a clue
But I'll always treasure my first review.

Heart

Heart.
The centre of our being, thought, feeling, emotion,
Our very essence or merely Harvey's prosaic, organic pump,
Essential, no doubt, but simply circulating
Lifeblood around our mortal frames?
Mine unquestioned and reliable,
Though metaphorically broken many times.

Until 28th November 2006, when three days shy of fifty.
Clutching at the doorframe, my sole support,
Alone as the earthquake struck,
Deep, shuddering shockwaves,
Tremors emanating from the epicentre of my chest.
Each both making my breath start
And threatening to end it.
Each jolt heralding potential oblivion.
Over in a matter of seconds, I suppose:
Ten at the most,
Conceivably the remainder of a lifetime.

Ashen and breathless,
Surprised, concerned but still in a hurry.
Living's a perpetual struggle to avoid being late,
That day no less than any other.
Two aspirins swallowed, just in case
That was how a heart attack feels.

There wasn't time for one of those.
Photos to take, making haste
To the arts centre,
Heavy bag shouldered,
Bowed but not beaten,
Weakened and weary but still able
To compose, focus and shoot.
Irony acknowledged: a barely discernible
Hint of a smile played on my blue-grey lips,

Recording Blake Drama Club's dress rehearsal of
Over My Dead Body,
So close to becoming the perfect prop.

Next stop A&E, you might surmise?
But no. Driving out onto the Levels,
Collecting friends and heading off
For a slap-up pre-birthday meal,
Gaviscon proffered, obediently consumed,
With no obvious signs of relief.

Despite such senseless neglect,
It did not prove to be the final meal
Of the self-condemned man.
Sometimes fortune favours the foolish,
Blockages occur millimetres from disaster,
And I lived to tell the tale.

Breaking News

I see them through the window.
Three small girls play and laugh
In the scent-filled garden,
Blissful in the mid-June sunshine,
Aged five, four and two.

Like a celluloid vision of idyllic childhood
With the director about to call 'Cut'.
A moment of sweet, unknowing innocence,
Which can never be re-created.

We call them in.
They sit together on the sofa,
Barely comprehending the news
We have to impart.

'Daddy's going to live in a flat.'

Auntie Kit Kat

I can't remember how it started.
Mum said she met her in town,
A woman who was a cook at the hospital
Where they both once worked.
Either mum invited her round
Or she invited herself.
There's no one left to ask now.

She was what the less sensitive would have termed 'An Old Maid'
And even the kindest then would have called 'A Little Old Lady'.
Every couple of months,
For years she used to visit us.
Dad would pick her up en route from work
And bring her home to Chirk.
Then she'd go back on the bus.

And every time she came
She'd bring us kids a gift.
It was always just the same
For me and for my sister Pat:
Red-and-white-banded and silver-wrapped,
A gloriously tasty Kit Kat.
Not Nestlé's but a Rowntree's product then –
Chocolate from Quaker, philanthropic men.

It didn't take long to re-christen her
'Auntie Kit Kat'.
Dad didn't need to call her Auntie.
To him she was, warmly, just 'Kit Kat'.
More formally known as Miss White.
I think her first name may have been May.
She would never dream of calling my parents
Anything other than
Mr. and Mrs. Beech.

Displaced to North Wales by Nazi bombs on Exeter,
She somehow never went away.
When she came round, according to Pat,
She'd take off her coat, but never her hat.
It was knitted or crocheted. I'd forgotten that.
She'd sit on our sofa, knitting all evening,
And regale us in her Devon tones
Of Exe river, ex-parents, ex-homes.

But most of all she'd talk
About the life she led in Wrexham.
The world revolved around her church in Poyser Street
In dear old Wrexham town.
I've looked it up on the internet
And it's long since been knocked down.

It seems they were Primitive Methodists,
Presumably spreading the word by pigeon-post
Before snail-mail was invented.
Thereafter, perhaps, sending out sermons
Strapped to their shells,
Leaving a trail of miniature red rubber bands ………

We heard all the excitements of the life
Of the minister and his wife,
Mr. and Mrs. Pope-Green.
Funny name for Methodists I've always thought:
More appropriate for Irish Catholic sorts.
Perhaps when he was appointed
There was a moment of madness in their Methodism.

There may have been wild parties
She just forgot to mention,
Without restraints or inhibitions.
But it would appear 'Auntie Kit Kat' lived happily
In a world of church jumble sales,
Bring-and-buys and crochet exhibitions.

I made her journey in reverse:
Three years studying in Exeter.
Later, I moved away from home for good
And never saw her again.
After dad died, we lost touch
And I'm truly sorry for that.

She must have died sometime in the eighties or nineties,
While I was somewhere else
Doing something else.

Well, now I've written you an extended elegy.
Were you another real-life Eleanor Rigby?
Your life so different from mine.
We've both been non-conformists,
In our totally different ways.
But my memories of you will always
Remain both affectionate
And confectionate.

In a League of Her Own

I've fallen for a woman I've come to adore,
Feelings explored in poems you may have heard before.
She's so kind, so gentle and sweet –
She's quite swept me off both of my feet.
But though love is oft portrayed as blind,
And she seems a kindred spirit,
Hold on just a minute –
There has to be a limit.
Please don't judge me as less than kind –
There's just one thing that's been preying on my mind.
It really shouldn't matter much to me at all
BUT my sweetheart knows sweet FA about football.

Now lots of women play and watch the game.
That's really great, of course, but it's such a crying shame
That my dearest darling doesn't feel the same.
Just imagine her dismay
When told there's games on every day.
It's just the modern way.
It never goes away –
TV pays and has its say and they must play.
There's such disinterest on her face.
She'd rather search for antique lace.

United are red, City are blue.
Other than that, she hasn't a clue.
And to tell you true,
She doesn't even know those two.
To her Toffees are sweets, she's not owned a rattle.
Stamford Bridge was just a very old battle.
The Cottage and Villa –
She don't know the score.
No six-goal thriller,
She's thinking charming house,
Roses entwined round the door.
And I'm starting to feel –
Or is it just me? –

If I mentioned Anfield
She'd ask 'Who is she?'
Surely you don't need a PhD?
But I'd Kop it alright
And I'd face that third degree.

Still, I'm crazy about her – she is quite a catch.
In so many ways my perfect non-football match.
BUT I have to proclaim
Without fear, without shame,
That I still feel the love that dare not speak its name.
Don't patronise me with smirks and with pity.
My first love will always remain
Stoke City.

Let me quickly assuage
Your scorn and your rage.
At least we both like Reading –
Er, no – that works better when seen on the page.
Yes, we share *other* tragic passions, never you fear.
We can both enjoy a Hamlet or Lear.
To literature she's not apathetic.
Aw well, at least she's heard of Wigan's Pier,
If not its Athletic.
But she'd find it very hard
To understand,
Be confused,
If not stunned,
By how a Black Cat's red card
Might be construed
As Malice in Sunderland.

It's on Radio 4 that we both thrive
But at critical moments I have to contrive
To sneak the dial round to Radio 5 Live.

We can both weep at the fate of fairest Cordelia
Or grieve at the grave of poor drown-ed Ophelia
But darling why can't you be just a bit more like Delia?

Of Carrow Road you've never heard.
To me it seems so absurd
That to you, a Magpie, Swan or Canary is merely a bird.
And it's a matter of the very greatest concern
That you are grimly determined not to learn.
Your attitude never varies –
Don't care who plays at the Hawthorns or St Mary's.
Just adding to my troubles
And causing further pain,
You don't care who's forever blowing bubbles
Or who's based at White Hart Lane.

Well, we'll have to share some other things
If we're ever to exchange those golden rings.
Oh, to alter me you'll get no clear-cut chance.
You'll come to see in our romance
That though I no longer fit
Inside my very ancient kit,
Please no moans or groans or gripes,
A Proud Potter can never lose his youthful stripes.

Perhaps begin by teaching me to knit long socks
And get me thinking just outside the box?
But however much you may implore,
You simply cannot ignore
That to Knit 1 Purl 1 is just a low scoring draw.
Sad for both you and me,
To you a long throw, it just covers your settee.
Oh, there's such an obvious penalty
For diving into love with me.

You smile, clasp hands around my expanded waist,
Bestow a tender kiss.
Oh, has it really come to this?
OK, you win, you've sprung my offside trap.
I know that I've been talking … rubbish.
You've broken down my defensive wall.
I've started to take my eye off the ball.
Just right now it doesn't really Juan Mata much at all.

47

Well, our interests may remain an eclectic mixture
But for me my love, home or away,
You've become a permanent fixture.
You see, yes, yes, yes it's true!
I love you just the way you are,
Even though it's simply quite bizarre,
You don't know your Arsenal from your QPR.

St. Valentine's Day Massager

When you grabbed the knob and turned on the power,
I thought we were in for a hot 'n' steamy half-hour,
Anticipating an exhilarating rollercoaster ride,
Your reservations, and clothing, both set aside.
I'd pleaded 'Don't worry. It'll be just fine.'
But with cold glass icing down your spine
And even colder tiles penetrating mine,
Squashed in far too tightly,
As usual, you were the one thinking rightly.
You weren't just making undue fuss.
This shower ain't big enough for the two of us.

Great Expectations

Heaven forfend,
Lest you conclude my love life's at an end,
But it has to be said
There **are** other things to do in bed.

Well, there's sleep of course.
That's natural, you'll surely endorse,
But there is another source
Of horizontal bliss,
Besides the bedtime 'kiss'.

I love this pursuit with the woman in my life
(We're not labelled as 'husband' and 'wife').
There's such consummate pleasure,
As we lie there together, enjoying our leisure,
All snuggle-bunnied tight,
Ready for the highlight of the night.

I hope my pressing need
You'll come to understand.
I simply have to read,
As I lie there with Longfellow or Hardy in my hand.
Inexplicably, she loves to hear my voice,
Making her my perfect choice.
I'm so anxious to perform
And to strut upon a stage,
And now it is her norm
To find it hard to hold and turn a page.
Residual illness has taken its toll,
So listening to books is now her favoured role.
Our late night escapades are more a case of literary win-win
Rather than any kind of bedroom 'sin'.

Our reading schedule's often quite hectic
And it's always been extremely eclectic.
Nigel Slater, Saint Roger McGough,

Carol Ann Duffy, Anton Chekhov.
Garrison Keiller's 'Lake Wobegon Days'
Always a wry smile will raise.
Set in the States, it doesn't seem the slightest bit foreign.
After all, it's always been a quiet week in Norton Fitzwarren.

Well, we don't do **everything** by the book.
At the end of chapter or verse,
She often gives me that special look
That intimates intentions only ever so slightly perverse.
We don't want to read **all** of the time.
After all, we're still relatively close to our prime.
I still love that sweet darling of mine
And our shared moments remain completely sublime.
Yes, sometimes she catches me right on the hop
And I return most gratefully to that fascinating Old Curiosity Shop.

And though I'm hardly counting my chickens,
Why she suggested just this week,
As we lay there cheek to cheek,
Maybe it's time we had another crack at Dickens.

Fantasy Novel

I'm tired of living in a hovel,
So I think I'll write myself a novel.
Then to an agent I will grovel,
Maybe in Taunton or in Yeov'l.
In life one has to take one's chances,
Grab those five-book deals and huge advances.
Oh, happy days and happy nights!
Once I've sold the world film rights.

Man Booker Prize and clutch of Oscars within reach,
I'd better prepare an acceptance speech.
'Behind every success there are so many crucial factors,
None more so than choosing perfect actors.'

For even if your cinematography glows,
As they speak your golden prose
And your screenplay clearly excels,
As every ad executive knows,
It's really sex that sells.

I need amazingly attractive actors of great fame
But it's such a dreadful shame,
I can't ever quite recall anybody's name.
People are often cruelly amused
That I get so awfully confused.

For my tale of love and loss, my modern day myth,
I'll need that charming hunk, for whom
All the women seem to swoon.
You know, one of those later Colins:
Colin Fourth or Colin Fifth.

And beside him in her rightful place,
The screen goddess with that face.
A perfect match for a Darcy or a Knightley,
Who, if I remember rightly,
Goes by the name of Kiera Daley.
Or is that just me?

Oh, I think I want to scream.
Seems it was only just a dream.
Here's hard fact not fantasy.
Plain truth for all to see.
My unwritten book is better dead
Than read.
So I think I'll stay in bed.

Flight of Fancy

My best mate rang me and Maria
But, just like this one,
It was a bad line.
I said 'He says he's fine
And I think he said he's going on holiday.'
'Don't call me with your latest poem of the day.
I'm seeing my new girlfriend, named Juliet.'
'Balcony seen?' … 'Great, it's always good to get
Initial embarrassment out of the way.'

'She's coming round very soon, on the early evening bus
And once she's here, I don't want you to interrupt us.
I'm hoping later we may end up in Flagrante.'
And he slammed the phone down.
Must be a last minute deal in that little town
Just outside of Alicante.
Mind you, Spain is lovely
At this time of year.

Estrangement

My oldest friend.
Comradeship destined to last
Right up until the end.
Just like our fathers before us,
Joined by a bond as strong
As consanguinity.

So what is this?
Another minor non-lovers' tiff?
Your somewhat insensitively phrased email,
Tentatively queried on the 'phone,
Prefaced by 'Don't take this the wrong way but',
A sentence obviously destined to fail.

Stunned by your decision to cut all ties,
Saddened beyond all words, with regretful sighs,
I still fail to comprehend
The vehemence of your reaction.
I may not quite yet have reached Falstaffian proportions
But banish me, and banish all the world.

Surely this cannot last?
Can fifty years be consigned
To the dust of history
Before the grave has intervened?
I saw your father wipe a tear from his eye
When my dad was lying in the morgue.
I saw your father as he lay helpless,
Close to breathing for the very last time.

Don't days, or weeks, or years from now,
Regret we never spoke again
Or come to my funeral full of pain
And think how our friendship had unravelled.

I'm missing the football.
Get on the 'phone again, you silly bastard,
And talk to me about all the really important things in life
Like Stoke City, Wolves (and will you finally have a wife?).

I'm so happy that you've found her
And I wish you both such joy.
But don't forget your oldest friend.
It's not too late for **us** to enjoy
Our ties so deep, close and rare
And that lifelong friendship
It's surely still our destiny to share.

Spell Check

How do you spell check?

Check   - In at the airport, or maybe on your shirt?

Cech   - In goal for Chelsea, diving in the dirt?

Check   - Out the talent, or where you have to pay?

Chek   - Hov in the theatre, if you want to see a play?

Cheque   - Put it in the bank or write a bouncing one?

Czech   - My girlfriend back in Prague, with whom I once had fun?

Well, how **do** you spell check?
If I get it wrong, I'll get it in the neck.
So I'd better turn my computer on
And well, you know, just check.

F1

Formula One, Formula One.
Is that your idea of having fun?
Chasing each other in flashy chariots
Seems simply archaic,
Not to mention,
Well, frankly, rather formulaic.
You seem to love each tedious lap
But I just think the whole things ... boring.
I'll more than likely soon be snoring,
As I'd much rather just go and have a nap.

Formula One, Formula One.
Can't wait until your race is run.
I think I'll go and put on the kettle.
I really cannot possibly settle
For watching boy racers in shiny metal
In vain pursuit of Sebastian Vettel.

OK, you say, they're not made of metal.
I don't care if it's carbon-fibre or fibreglass.
In fact, I couldn't really give a ... damn.
It's all your heart desires
To see them changing all their tyres,
Wearing fireproof mitts
But to me it's just the pits.
It's really getting on my ... nerves.

Whether you're on wet-weather or shiny slicks,
I had more fun as a kid with Scalectrix.
No wonder your 'sport' is called Grand Prix.
You see, rich kids in fast cars,
They just don't do it for me.
My heart races to the beat of fast-paced poetry.
Watching Ralf and Michael Schumacher
Was always highly over-rated.
After all, that's just a pair of cobblers when it's translated.

Formula One, Formula One.
It's still on. When will it be done?
I can't believe you're still having fun.
It's your idea of heaven
Even on Lap Forty-Bleeding-Seven.
For this stuff you're such a glutton
But it doesn't push my Jensen Button.
Yes for me, my spirits start to sag
Countless hours before
That longed-for chequered flag.

Formula One, Formula One.
I'm not violent but sometimes
I wish I had a gun.
I feel such a sense of odium
When you step onto the podium.
It's such a crying shame
That you waste so much Champagne,
Like so many wastrel bankers.
I think you're all a load of over-privileged … playboys.
Seems to me you're all just on the pull.
Red or any other colour, it's such a load of macho bull.

Formula One, Formula One,
Crossing the globe, chasing the sun.
But to me you won't easily explain
Why you race in iffy places like Bahrain.
Monaco, Monza, Silverstone,
They just chill me to the bone.
Hockenheim or Nürburgring,
They don't mean a thing.
In fact, it may sound somewhat circuitous
But I only like one track –
And that's the one by Fleetwood Mac.
It'll take more than a quick snatch of 'Rumours'
To restore me to more pleasant humours.

Formula One, Formula One.
I think my rant is nearly done.
Why, oh why can't you just go and F1?
F-ing, F-ing Formula One.

Love Match of the Day

Following a close encounter,
There was a precious away win
In the I-Love-You local derby.
Final Score:
I-Love-You Dear   1-2   I-Love-You.

Ashes Haiku

Australia bat
Anderson, Broad, Stokes and Finn
Won't take long to win.

Trent Bridge First Innings Haiku

Nought, nought, six, nought, ten,
One, two, thirteen, one, four, nine,
Extras fourteen. OUT!

Killer Seagulls Eat Ducklings

Please don't say you're unimpressed
By some of my work. Don't make me depressed.
Photographing for local and regional press,
Journals renowned for reportage at its exceptional best
And not at all prone to sensational excess.

Imagine my excitement,
For hope is quite eternal,
When I saw the poster advertising a March copy
Of that august journal,
Outside Norton Fitzwarren's premier outlet.
That Titan of the Press,
More or less:
The Somerset County Gazette.

Now, I shouldn't bite the hand that feeds me.
Well, pays for the occasional part main meal –
That's just one Weetabix I feel,
Rather than my customary three.

BUT what was on the poster on that aptly named board?
'KILLER SEAGULLS EAT DUCKLINGS'.
Yes, you may well laugh and scoff.
This seagull story's not penned by Chekhov.

But it's bound to have the village running to the store
Desperate to learn more and more
And read the full story of this avian gore.
Some of the sicker minds –
Every community has its more violent kinds –
Will be hoping it's a DVD,
A kind of feather-flying fluff-snuff movie.
The sort that they would love to see,
Not available even on non-terrestrial TV
And certainly not endorsed by the RSPB.

And what of the RSPB?
How does it view such bird on bird activity?
What can it do about all that hate?
Seagull detention to rehabilitate?
Protect the remaining ducklings before it's too late
Or 'duckling dans le bec' will be their fate.

Back to the poster,
Encouraging readers to 'Have your say online'.
Well, democracy's all well and fine
But who the hell has got the time?
Unlike the poor ducklings in their strife,
Such virtual pundits should just 'Get a Life'.
This assault of gull on duck,
Don't tell me that you give a … care
Or perhaps your thoughts you'd like to share?
Maybe I should join in, while I'm in the humour,
Spread my own ill-founded rumour?
After all, it can't be all that hard
To write my own tasty little canard.

Still I really cannot wait
For next week's paper to come through
With the sequel to this great debate.
So what will the park authorities do?
Can the ducklings retaliate?
For behaviour so deleterious
This time it's serious:
'KILLER DUCKLINGS EAT SEAGULLS TOO'.

Rex Marks the Spot

Fortunately, it's not every day
One stumbles over a Richard III in a car park ...

So imagine my surprise
When before my very eyes ...
I was totally agog
When they found Shakespeare's 'bloody dog'.
The one we all so love to hate,
Well, most of us at any rate.
No one knew exact details of his fate,
As he'd gone strangely AWOL just of late.
It sounds so utterly absurd
But they've found that dastardly Dick,
That wretched Richard
Sequentially named 'The Third'.

Long gone – but not forgotten,
Though his body's well past rotten.
Reviled, detested and disgraced
But for centuries, curiously misplaced.

This is a melancholy tale
Of malevolent majesty uncovered and laid bare.
The man against whom our greatest bard did rail,
Now looking rather worse for wear.

But soft, our story now unfolds ...

He was hacked down on Bosworth Field upon that August day.
August no more, as history had its say.
Decrowned, disrobed, dishonoured, dead and bundled on a horse
By Henry VII – he was the victor there, of course.
Well, Henry wasn't one to let things fester,
So he dumped defeated Dick in a future car park back in Leicester.

It was a church in those days,
Back in the mists of time,
When the friars were in their prime.
A sanctified home for the leader of an evil junta,
The most famous inmate of Grey Friars – prior
To the birth of Billy Bunter.

Time marches on.
Now the friars themselves are gone,
Victims of monasterial decline,
Aka Henry VIII's gold mine,
Their walls and flesh dissolved and with them any trace
Of royal Richard's resting place.
No Rex marks the spot
In the future parking lot.

Fast forward to 2012.
A Leicester City Council car park, where it's time to delve.
Rumours abound – Is he here? Is he there?
Was he moved? Do we care?
Will we ever know the truth?
Perhaps discover concrete proof?
There are so many tales, legends as apocryphal as Noah's Ark,
In this veritable multi-story car park.

A skeleton uncovered, roughly laid to rest,
Bearing wounds to head and chest,
To name but few,
And with spinal curvature clear to view.
Science will have its way,
Revealing secrets day by day.

Early 2013. Speculation's rife –
'Thank God he's really male' –
And everyone is tense.
The camping shops are cashing in, true to life,
With an early springtime sale:
'Now is the discount of our winter tents'.

Male, early thirties, violent death back 500 years or more.
Facial reconstruction and DNA
May prove things either way.
If there's a match, we'll finally know the score.

Wow! There's proof beyond the merest doubt,
As ever more conclusive facts keep spilling out.

Half a millennium underground.
That's one hell of a long stay car park.
Good job the council hasn't got a TARDIS
To slap on retrospective charges.
Imagine a medieval jobsworth …
'Not within a clearly marked bay.'
He'd surely have to pay.
And now it's proved that his spine
Was somewhat out of line,
There's bound to be a fine.
The plot grows thicker –
'Failure to display a disabled sticker.'

If only we could resurrect that great dramatist without equal,
Perhaps he could bring us up to speed with a fascinating sequel.
A working title? Well, not too original but I suppose it'll have to do.
He could just try something simple, like 'Richard III Part Two'.

What would Tricky Dicky think if he only knew?
His mortal bones on worldwide view,
Subjected to laboratory test
And still not finally laid to rest.

Fear not, a new home awaits this king,
Medieval gangster or wrongly much maligned.
Will like his bones, his reputation be realigned?
If he really killed the Princes in the Tower
Well, that was not his finest hour.
The things men will do for power.
They really don't impress.

But ... I digress.
A new burial planned for 2014 –
529 years late it would seem.
In Leicester Cathedral he'll take his place,
Less in haste, perhaps less in disgrace?
Is that a smile playing on his face?

So just remember when struck by bad fortune's sideways glance
It's never too late for a second chance.
Remember I've recorded here in verse,
Things could always, always be much worse.
Put your own reputation into reverse.
'A hearse, a hearse, my kingdom for a hearse.'

Origin of Class and Order, Not Species

I've been thinking about etymology.
I wanted to think about the study of insects
But I didn't know how to spell it.
Anyway, since I'm here,
I wonder where the word 'insect' comes from?

I've been thinking about entomology.
I wanted to think about the origin of words
But I didn't know how to spell it.
Anyway, since I'm here,
I wonder if 'beetle' comes from the Scouse for singer?

Rodney
(after *Nothing Happens Now I'm Old*
By Rodney Bowsher)

Nothing's quite the same now you're gone.
I never knew you when you were young
Or during your multifarious careers
But I remember
Meeting you and Lorraine at the Phoenix
And hearing you perform that first time,
A typically hilarious set,
Deadpan delivery,
Taking the Mic for all you were worth.

Nothing's quite the same now you're gone.
But I remember
Shaking your hand, then watching that hand shake,
As you stood and outscored me in the slam,
Your fingers trembling, struggling to separate
The pages that bore your clever words.

Nothing's quite the same now you're gone.
But I remember
Your only visit for lunch
And the dedication you wrote for us
In our copy of *Book Ends*,
A book full of poetic smiles
And poignant reflections
On what was yet to come,
And soon.

Nothing's quite the same now you're gone.
But I remember
The last time I saw you perform,
Increasingly frail,
The prolonged shuffle to the stage
Before proving you'd still got it,
A trooper to the last.

Nothing's quite the same now you're gone.
But I remember
Reading *Hospital*
To your poetry friends,
Your beautifully observed
Description of the place in which you lay.

Nothing's quite the same now you're gone.
But I remember
That last hospital conversation,
Holding your hand
And hearing you say
'Just be yourself.'

Nothing's quite the same now you're gone.
But I remember
Reading your poems to you,
That one last time,
Believing you heard
And your own words brought comfort.

Nothing's quite the same now you're gone.
But I remember
Reading your *Head in the Clouds*
As we mourned you
At the end of your show.

No, nothing's quite the same now you're gone.
But I remember.
We all remember,
Offering Lorraine our love and support.
We remember you
And we remember your words:
So no giving up. And because I tried,
I never died; I never died.

Lima Bound

Overnight coach to Heathrow,
Too excited for sleep,
Gathering for the trip of our lifetimes.
Striking Parkinson's pink tee-shirts ablaze at 5a.m.,
Advertising the charitable cause
But doing little to calm our senses.

Every long journey begins with a single step.
On this occasion, strangely backwards,
Heading East, London to Amsterdam,
To fly West to South America,
Like an airborne game of
Snakes and ladders.
Our mid-air lives entrusted
To three mid-alphabet letters:
K, L and M,
Aboard Boeing 777 'Machu Picchu',
Its namesake our ultimate goal.

Notable landmarks along the route
Include the mighty Andes,
The Amazon Basin
And Brentford FC,
Not necessarily in that order,
But all majestic in their own right.
To be strictly accurate, Brentford's
Griffin Park seen below on our return,
Thus proving I may not qualify
For a pilot's licence
But I'm perfectly happy to employ
A poetic equivalent.

Watching and listening to Don Giovanni,
Mozart at 37,000 feet,
The divine at heavenly altitude,
Hurtling across the Atlantic Ocean.

Savouring that sublime libertine,
Dragged down into Hell,
In my own personal seven mile-high music club.
Our journey plotted on screen,
Complete with data confounding the brain:
External air temperature minus 50°C,
With 6,000 miles to fly, give or take.

Adrenalin surge as we reach the coast,
Long-imagined most of my fifty-one years.
Land I never dreamt I would see,
Now over-flown.
The photographer's obsession:
Creating a visual record,
Crossing the threshold of South America,
Door-stepping a continent from above.

Endless tracts of Amazonian rainforest,
A myriad meandering silver-ribbon courses
Anaconda-twist, punctuating the verdant canopy
That stretches beyond the horizon:
The alveoli of the earth.
Mystical, magical landscape,
Shrinking by the day,
Besieged by loggers and ranchers,
Human greed and self-harming insensitivity.
(I'm duly conscious of our own
Less-than-carbon-neutral flight overhead).

Rising over condor-swirled peaks,
Remote, savage and unyielding,
Before a sheering drop to sea level
And touchdown in Lima.

Then setting foot on South American concrete,
As momentous for me as Neil Armstrong,
With his one small step for man,
Mine most definitely in Peru,
His allegedly on the moon.
My greatest adventure had truly begun.

Appearances Can Be Deceptive

Anticipation,
Weaving through
the urban sprawl
Of Lima by coach,
From the airport
To our downtown hotel,
Anxious to catch first glimpse
Of the great Pacific Ocean.

We enter a long, narrow street,
Edging towards the sea.
Looking ahead, at the end of the road
I see a small patch of blue water.
'There it is, the Pacific Ocean!
Funny, I'd always thought it would be
Much larger than that.'

On the Road to Ollantaytambo

Flown high over Andean peaks,
Snow-capped, jagged shards
Piercing the ice-cold air,
From Lima to Cusco by Star Perú jet,
Tail and rudder festooned
With appropriately uplifting art,
From sea level to heady altitude:
3,400 metres above the ocean.

Apprehension as we step
From the plane into thin air …
Free oxygen cylinders
Both reassure and unnerve,
As we tentatively queue for our bags.
Relief that breathing comes easy,
Triggering an impromptu dancing display:
Modern jive with attitude at altitude,
Accompanied by the indigenous pipes and guitar
Of musicians with CDs to sell.
Inadvisable exhibitionism, no doubt,
But expressing the sheer joy of breathing
And simply being alive.

Some of us buy authentic woollen goods
As we climb on the coach,
From a young, blue-sun-hatted woman.
Her charm and striking good looks
Have remained in my memory for years.

Off to the Cross Keys bar,
In Cusco's historic main square,
For compulsory coca tea.
I've lived a sheltered life: I don't do coke,
Or even pepsi.
But this is purely medicinal,
The ancient herbal remedy claimed to avert
The dangers of altitude sickness,
Though not fully guaranteed to succeed.

A few seconds of room-swimming blur in the bar,
Then I'm fine for the rest of the trip,
Legs, lungs and by-passed heart up to the test
Of the precipitous trekking to come.

Back on the coach, snaking north-west
Through high mountain passes,
Driven close to the edge.
A frisson of high adventure
On the road to Ollantaytambo,
Where the Incas defeated the Spaniards
Nearly half a millennium ago.
Manco Inca's victory
Merely delaying eventual defeat,
Imperialists terrorising the globe,
Exploiting resources and people,
Much as they still do today.

We pull into a lay-by,
High above the valley floor,
Surrounded by towering summits.
Patchworks of snow trimming gullies,
Tenacious and stubborn,
They cling and glint
In the dazzling sunshine
Of this perfect afternoon.

We buy bottled water
And peruse Peruvian textiles,
Proffered by patient local traders,
All women,
A glittering array of pulsing colours
Seducing the senses:
Shawls, rugs, hats, gloves,
Purses, bags, dolls and more,
Traditionally woven in time-honoured
Classic designs, llamas and condors
Proclaiming Peru to the world.

Destined to travel to every continent
In the rucksacks and cases
Of the trekkers and tourists
Who paw at the goods.

And with the women,
As they genially trade,
A small girl, five years old,
Or maybe six,
Gloriously wrapped in scarlet-and-gold-striped cloak,
Complementing her jet-black hair,
Standing proud, innocent and inquisitive
Close to her mother's side.
For me the essence of childhood,
Dignity and real hope for the world,
Encapsulated in one small Peruvian frame.

She gazes steadily across the sea of textiles
As I carefully press the shutter release.
A photograph taken,
A moment captured,
Never to be forgotten.
A vision encountered
On a high Andes pass
On the road to Ollantaytambo
In October 2008.

James

Have you read James Turner's poem *Simply Alive*
Or better still heard him read it from the heart,
In soft, measured tones, imploring us
To see the beauty of our lives?

Seek out his work and embrace it,
As he embraces each of us
And defy a tear to form.
Hard won knowledge from one who shares
The pain so long endured,
Without self-pity,
Such exquisite explorations
Of wounds that linger deep within.

And he's funny too. You'll notice.
A gentle man enriching our lives
With his wit, wisdom and unfailing honesty,
Gladdening our hearts
As purveyor of botany's also-rans:
Weed of the Week on Facebook.
A lover of life and the natural world,
Confronting his past
And offering hope to us all.

Thank you, James, for the reminder
That *'Life is enough in itself'*
And that we are all *'utterly beautiful'*,
None of us more so than you.

Power Cut

Forced out of our medieval warren
In search of sustenance.
Western Power Distribution blitzing our street,
A phalanx of hi-vis yellows and hard hats,
Depriving us of current all day,
With the promise of updated and better to come.
From South to North,
Strung out and stringing up
Sinuous black cables, as thick as your wrist.

Heading to Ashton's Coffee Lounge
In uptown Crediton,
For coffees, bagels and baguettes.
Overlooking the square,
Surrounded by the happy chatter
Of school-liberated children,
Marshalling mothers
And a smattering of
Twenty-first century dads,
On the first Thursday of the Easter break.

Irrespective of electrical interference,
We must do this again.

For Iris and Terry

Carpe Diem

Sitting in a Somerset garden,
Birdsong filling the air,
Relaxed in the company of friends
Of twenty years and more,
So glad to see them again.

Birthday card and bottle of red
Ceremoniously transferred
To Terry, claiming now
To be three quarters,
Of a century, that is.
Still as robust, sharp and amusing
As the years keep winging by.

Before we leave, he gives us a tour,
Of the garden he and Iris have fashioned
Through decades of hard grafting,
Tender, loving cultivation
And boundless imagination.
Hedges, pergolas, arches,
Creating distinctive compartments
Of burgeoning, horticultural joy.

A smile of remembrance
By the small garden chalet,
Where, though over-excited,
My three girls slept through
A whole balmy night,
So many summers ago.

Today, there's hopeful late April blossom,
Presaging hot, cloudless afternoons
And scent-filled evenings to savour
In the long-lit months ahead.

And as we pass the two tall,
Gnarled, contorted hazels,
Once planted as saplings,
We startle two blackbirds,
A mated pair,
Post-brood companions,
Concealed in a bush.

They thrash over the path
And thud into unseen panes,
He bounces off and disappears,
While she silent and still remains,
Lodged in the pyracantha
Below the kitchen window,
Tiny feet uppermost.

Iris lifts the fragile frame,
Soft and warm,
Lifeless in her palm.
Neck broken,
Life extinguished,
Cut short,
In an instant,
So unexpectedly,
On a sunny afternoon.

We say our goodbyes,
Propose our next meeting,
And drive away chastened,
Determined to seize
The remains of the day.

For Emily, Grace and Megan

Turners

In the National Gallery
With all of my daughters.
What a delight.
Marvelling at Ulysses leaving the Cyclops behind,
The Fighting Temeraire
And the train in the rain,
Steaming across the viaduct.

Three priceless, consummate works of art,
All distinctly different, each radiating
Glorious light and reflections,
Lovingly created in a past
That is now a far distant country,
Filling my heart with joy,
As they stand admiring the Turners.

Notes

Page 23   An earlier version of *Late* appeared in *WalnutCrackers: an anthology* edited by Robert Garnham.

Page 27   An earlier version of *Capitalism for Beginners in Lingua Franca* appeared in *WalnutCrackers: an anthology* edited by Robert Garnham.

Page 29   *Small Arms* was written after reading *As Used On the Famous Nelson Mandela* by Mark Thomas.

Page 41   An earlier version of *Breaking News* appeared in *WalnutCrackers: an anthology* edited by Robert Garnham.

Page 42   Names in *Auntie Kit Kat*, based on very hazy memories, need further research when time allows.

Page 45   *In a League of Her Own* includes references to all twenty teams in the top flight of English men's football during the 2012-2013 season. There is no prize for identifying them all.

Page 55   *F1* was written before the tragic skiing accident of Michael Schumacher. The author's thoughts are with him and his family, with best wishes for his continuing recovery.

Page 57   Haiku written with grateful thanks to the Australian men's cricket team for their abysmal batting performances in the Ashes Tests at Edgbaston and Trent Bridge, July and August 2015.

Page 64   *Rodney* was written in tribute to much-loved Devon poet Rodney Bowsher, who sadly died in September 2014. The poems mentioned all appear in Rodney's book *Book Ends*, published just a few short months before his death.

Page 69   The cover photo of this book, referred to in *On the Road to Ollantaytambo*, was taken on 5th October 2008.

Page 72   *James* celebrates the poetry of James Turner in general but was written after reading his poem *Simply Alive* in *WalnutCrackers: an anthology* edited by Robert Garnham.

About the Author

Ian Beech, born in North Wales, moved to Crediton in Devon in 2014, having lived in Somerset for twenty years. Freelance photographer, former public librarian, now part-time school library worker, Ian's lifelong love of books, literature and the spoken word has been reinvigorated by the success of his youngest daughter, performance poet and author Megan. Taking Megan to her first gigs inspired him to write and perform himself, and he's delighted to have performed on the same bill as her on several occasions to date.

He performs his poetry at a wide range of events, several times every month. Some are regular slots at events in Taunton (Fire River Poets), Exeter (both Uncut Poets & Taking the Mic) and Torquay (Poetry Island) and occasionally at The Bike Shed in Exeter. He has performed for Apples and Snakes at Forked! in Plymouth and was runner-up in the 2014 Exeter Poetry Slam. Ian has also performed at The Poetry Café at The Poetry Society in London, Cross Country Writers in Plymouth, Totnes Poetry Collective, Rhymewarp in Plymouth, The Artizan Gallery in Torquay, The Royal Albert Memorial Museum in Exeter (for the RSPB), Poetry Cafe in Tiverton, the Cheltenham Poetry Festival, and numerous poetry festivals throughout the South West.

In September 2014 Ian became the new host and organiser of Torquay's renowned Poetry Island at The Blue Walnut Cafe, where he's delighted to present top-class performance poetry every month, from highly talented local poets and star headliners alike. His new monthly poetry radio show, Poetry Islanders, launched on 28 June 2015 on Soundart Radio at Dartington.

In 2014 he also branched out into stand-up comedy, performing well received sets at both the Jocular Spectacular Roving Comedy Club and at The Artizan Gallery in Torquay and making his debut as a wedding reception entertainer.

For more information about Ian's poetry, Poetry Islanders, Poetry Island and other forthcoming events please visit:

www.ianbeechpoetry.com   www.mixcloud.com/PoetryIslanders/

www.facebook.com/pages/POETRY-ISLAND/